Great Works

Instructional Guides for Literature

The Stories Julian Tells

A guide for the book by Ann Cameron
Great Works Author: Melissa Callaghan

SHELL EDUCATION

Publishing Credits

Robin Erickson, *Production Director*; Lee Aucoin, *Creative Director*; Timothy J. Bradley, *Illustration Manager*; Emily R. Smith, M.A.Ed., *Editorial Director*; Amber Goff, *Editorial Assistant*; Don Tran, *Production Supervisor*; Corinne Burton, M.A.Ed., *Publisher*

Image Credits

Cover image Samuel Borges Photography/Shutterstock

Standards

© 2007 Teachers of English to Speakers of Other Languages, Inc. (TESOL)
© 2007 Board of Regents of the University of Wisconsin System. World-Class Instructional Design and Assessment (WIDA)
© Copyright 2010. National Governors Association Center for Best Practices and Council of Chief State School Officers. All rights reserved.

Shell Education

5301 Oceanus Drive
Huntington Beach, CA 92649-1030
http://www.shelleducation.com
ISBN 978-1-4258-8971-5
© 2014 Shell Educational Publishing, Inc.

Table of Contents

How to Use This Literature Guide

Today's standards demand rigor and relevance in the reading of complex texts. The units in this series guide teachers in a rich and deep exploration of worthwhile works of literature for classroom study. The most rigorous instruction can also be interesting and engaging!

Many current strategies for effective literacy instruction have been incorporated into these instructional guides for literature. Throughout the units, text-dependent questions are used to determine comprehension of the book as well as student interpretation of the vocabulary words. The books chosen for the series are complex and are exemplars of carefully crafted works of literature. Close reading is used throughout the units to guide students toward revisiting the text and using textual evidence to respond to prompts orally and in writing. Students must analyze the story elements in multiple assignments for each section of the book. All of these strategies work together to rigorously guide students through their study of literature.

The next few pages will make clear how to use this guide for a purposeful and meaningful literature study. Each section of this guide is set up in the same way to make it easier for you to implement the instruction in your classroom.

Theme Thoughts

The great works of literature used throughout this series have important themes that have been relevant to people for many years. Many of the themes will be discussed during the various sections of this instructional guide. However, it would also benefit students to have independent time to think about the key themes of the book.

Before students begin reading, have them complete the *Pre-Reading Theme Thoughts* (page 13). This graphic organizer will allow students to think about the themes outside the context of the story. They'll have the opportunity to evaluate statements based on important themes and defend their opinions. Be sure to keep students' papers for comparison to the *Post-Reading Theme Thoughts* (page 59). This graphic organizer is similar to the pre-reading activity. However, this time, students will be answering the questions from the point of view of one of the characters in the book. They have to think about how the character would feel about each statement and defend their thoughts. To conclude the activity, have students compare what they thought about the themes before the book to what the characters discovered during the story.

How to Use This Literature Guide (cont.)

Vocabulary

Each teacher reference vocabulary overview page has definitions and sentences about how key vocabulary words are used in the section. These words should be introduced and discussed with students. Students will use these words in different activities throughout the book.

On some of the vocabulary student pages, students are asked to answer text-related questions about vocabulary words from the sections. The following question stems will help you create your own vocabulary questions if you'd like to extend the discussion.

- How does this word describe _____'s character?
- How does this word connect to the problem in this story?
- How does this word help you understand the setting?
- Tell me how this word connects to the main idea of this story.
- What visual pictures does this word bring to your mind?
- Why do you think the author used this word?

At times, you may find that more work with the words will help students understand their meanings and importance. These quick vocabulary activities are a good way to further study the words.

- Students can play vocabulary concentration. Make one set of cards that have the words on them and another set with the definitions. Then, have students lay them out on the table and play concentration. The goal of the game is to match vocabulary words with their definitions. For early readers or English language learners, the sets of cards could be the words and pictures of the words.
- Students can create word journal entries about the words. Students choose words they think are important and then describe why they think each word is important within the book. Early readers or English language learners could instead draw pictures about the words in a journal.
- Students can create puppets and use them to act out the vocabulary words from the stories. Students may also enjoy telling their own character-driven stories using vocabulary words from the original stories.

How to Use This Literature Guide (cont.)

Analyzing the Literature

After you have read each section with students, hold a small-group or whole-class discussion. Provided on the teacher reference page for each section are leveled questions. The questions are written at two levels of complexity to allow you to decide which questions best meet the needs of your students. The Level 1 questions are typically less abstract than the Level 2 questions. These questions are focused on the various story elements, such as character, setting, and plot. Be sure to add further questions as your students discuss what they've read. For each question, a few key points are provided for your reference as you discuss the book with students.

Reader Response

In today's classrooms, there are often great readers who are below average writers. So much time and energy is spent in classrooms getting students to read on grade level that little time is left to focus on writing skills. To help teachers include more writing in their daily literacy instruction, each section of this guide has a literature-based reader response prompt. Each of the three genres of writing is used in the reader responses within this guide: narrative, informative/explanatory, and opinion. Before students write, you may want to allow them time to draw pictures related to the topic. Book-themed writing paper is provided on pages 69–70 if your students need more space to write.

Guided Close Reading

Within each section of this guide, it is suggested that you closely reread a portion of the text with your students. Page numbers are given, but since some versions of the books may have different page numbers, the sections to be reread are described by location as well. After rereading the section, there are a few text-dependent questions to be answered by students. A graphic organizer has been provided to help students prepare for the group discussion. They should record their thoughts and ideas on the graphic organizer and refer to it during your discussion. Rather than just taking notes, you may want to require students to write complete responses to the questions before discussing them with you.

Encourage students to read one question at a time and then go back to the text and discover the answer. Work with students to ensure that they use the text to determine their answers rather than making unsupported inferences. Suggested answers are provided in the answer key.

How to Use This Literature Guide (cont.)

Guided Close Reading (cont.)

The generic open-ended stems below can be used to write your own text-dependent questions if you would like to give students more practice.

- What words in the story support . . . ?
- What text helps you understand . . . ?
- Use the book to tell why _____ happens.
- Based on the events in the story, . . . ?
- Show me the part in the text that supports . . . .
- Use the text to tell why . . . .

Making Connections

The activities in this section help students make cross-curricular connections to mathematics, science, social studies, fine arts, or other curricular areas. These activities require higher-order thinking skills from students but also allow for creative thinking.

Language Learning

A special section has been set aside to connect the literature to language conventions. Through these activities, students will have opportunities to practice the conventions of standard English grammar, usage, capitalization, and punctuation.

Story Elements

It is important to spend time discussing what the common story elements are in literature. Understanding the characters, setting, plot, and theme can increase students' comprehension and appreciation of the story. If teachers begin discussing these elements in early childhood, students will more likely internalize the concepts and look for the elements in their independent reading. Another very important reason for focusing on the story elements is that students will be better writers if they think about how the stories they read are constructed.

In the story elements activities, students are asked to create work related to the characters, setting, or plot. Consider having students complete only one of these activities. If you give students a choice on this assignment, each student can decide to complete the activity that most appeals to him or her. Different intelligences are used so that the activities are diverse and interesting to all students.

How to Use This Literature Guide (cont.)

Culminating Activity

At the end of this instructional guide is a creative culminating activity that allows students the opportunity to share what they've learned from reading the book. This activity is open ended so that students can push themselves to create their own great works within your language arts classroom.

Comprehension Assessment

The questions in this section require students to think about the book they've read as well as the words that were used in the book. Some questions are tied to quotations from the book to engage students and require them to think about the text as they answer the questions.

Response to Literature

Finally, students are asked to respond to the literature by drawing pictures and writing about the characters and stories. A suggested rubric is provided for teacher reference.

Correlation to the Standards

Shell Education is committed to producing educational materials that are research and standards based. In this effort, we have correlated all of our products to the academic standards of all 50 United States, the District of Columbia, the Department of Defense Dependents Schools, and all Canadian provinces.

Purpose and Intent of Standards

Standards are designed to focus instruction and guide adoption of curricula. Standards are statements that describe the criteria necessary for students to meet specific academic goals. They define the knowledge, skills, and content students should acquire at each level. Standards are also used to develop standardized tests to evaluate students' academic progress. Teachers are required to demonstrate how their lessons meet standards. Standards are used in the development of all of our products, so educators can be assured they meet high academic standards.

How To Find Standards Correlations

To print a customized correlation report of this product for your state, visit our website at http://www.shelleducation.com and follow the online directions. If you require assistance in printing correlation reports, please contact Customer Service at 1-877-777-3450.

Correlation to the Standards (cont.)

Standards Correlation Chart

The lessons in this guide were written to support the Common Core College and Career Readiness Anchor Standards. This chart indicates which sections of this guide address the anchor standards.

Common Core College and Career Readiness Anchor Standard	Section
CCSS.ELA-Literacy.CCRA.R.1—Read closely to determine what the text says explicitly and to make logical inferences from it; cite specific textual evidence when writing or speaking to support conclusions drawn from the text.	Guided Close Reading Sections 1–5; Making Connections Section 2; Story Elements Sections 2–3
CCSS.ELA-Literacy.CCRA.R.2—Determine central ideas or themes of a text and analyze their development; summarize the key supporting details and ideas.	Analyzing the Literature Sections 1–5; Theme Thoughts
CCSS.ELA-Literacy.CCRA.R.3—Analyze how and why individuals, events, or ideas develop and interact over the course of a text.	Analyzing the Literature Sections 1–5; Story Elements Section 1
CCSS.ELA-Literacy.CCRA.R.4—Interpret words and phrases as they are used in a text, including determining technical, connotative, and figurative meanings, and analyze how specific word choices shape meaning or tone.	Guided Close Reading Section 1; Language Learning Section 1
CCSS.ELA-Literacy.CCRA.R.5—Analyze the structure of texts, including how specific sentences, paragraphs, and larger portions of the text (e.g., a section, chapter, scene, or stanza) relate to each other and the whole.	Post-Reading Response to Literature
CCSS.ELA-Literacy.CCRA.R.10—Read and comprehend complex literary and informational texts independently and proficiently.	Post-Reading Theme Thoughts; Post-Reading Response to Literature
CCSS.ELA-Literacy.CCRA.W.1—Write arguments to support claims in an analysis of substantive topics or texts using valid reasoning and relevant and sufficient evidence.	Reader Response Sections 2, 5; Post-Reading Theme Thoughts
CCSS.ELA-Literacy.CCRA.W.2—Write informative/explanatory texts to examine and convey complex ideas and information clearly and accurately through the effective selection, organization, and analysis of content.	Reader Response Section 3; Story Elements Section 2
CCSS.ELA-Literacy.CCRA.W.3—Write narratives to develop real or imagined experiences or events using effective technique, well-chosen details and well-structured event sequences.	Reader Response Sections 1, 4; Story Elements Sections 2–3
CCSS.ELA-Literacy.CCRA.W.4—Produce clear and coherent writing in which the development, organization, and style are appropriate to task, purpose, and audience.	Story Elements Section 3; Making Connections Section 5

Correlation to the Standards (cont.)

Standards Correlation Chart (cont.)

Common Core College and Career Readiness Anchor Standard	Section
CCSS.ELA-Literacy.CCRA.L.1—Demonstrate command of the conventions of standard English grammar and usage when writing or speaking.	Making Connections Sections 1, 5; Story Elements Sections 1–3, 5; Language Learning Section 2–4
CCSS.ELA-Literacy.CCRA.L.2—Demonstrate command of the conventions of standard English capitalization, punctuation, and spelling when writing.	Making Connections 1, 5; Story Elements 1, 3, 5; Language Learning Section 5
CCSS.ELA-Literacy.CCRA.L.3—Apply knowledge of language to understand how language functions in different contexts, to make effective choices for meaning or style, and to comprehend more fully when reading or listening.	Guided Close Reading Sections 1–5; Language Learning Section 1
CCSS.ELA-Literacy.CCRA.L.4—Determine or clarify the meaning of unknown and multiple-meaning words and phrases by using context clues, analyzing meaningful word parts, and consulting general and specialized reference materials, as appropriate.	Vocabulary Sections 1–5
CCSS.ELA-Literacy.CCRA.L.5—Demonstrate understanding of figurative language, word relationships, and nuances in word meanings.	Guided Close Reading Sections 1–5; Language Learning Section 1
CCSS.ELA-Literacy.CCRA.L.6—Acquire and use accurately a range of general academic and domain-specific words and phrases sufficient for reading, writing, speaking, and listening at the college and career readiness level; demonstrate independence in gathering vocabulary knowledge when encountering an unknown term important to comprehension or expression.	Vocabulary Sections 1–5

TESOL and WIDA Standards

The lessons in this book promote English language development for English language learners. The following TESOL and WIDA English Language Development Standards are addressed through the activities in this book:

- **Standard 1:** English language learners communicate for social and instructional purposes within the school setting.

- **Standard 2:** English language learners communicate information, ideas and concepts necessary for academic success in the content area of language arts.

About the Author—Ann Cameron

Ann Cameron was born in 1943. She grew up on a farm near Rice Lake, Wisconsin, where she spent a lot of time exploring the outdoors. As a child, Cameron loved to read and decided in the third grade that she wanted to be a writer. She wanted to tell stories about children and their feelings. She hoped to write about the adventures children have, even if they are in their own imaginations.

Cameron attended Harvard University in Cambridge, Massachusetts. She studied history, psychology, writing, art, and literature. She did many interesting jobs in the world of publishing and eventually ended up living in Panajachel, Guatemala. Her time there changed her a great deal, and she devoted over 15 years to helping the town library so that the children would have access to many books. The Panajachel Library is now the largest library in Central America with over 15,000 books. She now lives in Portland, Oregon, but continues to help the town of Panajachel.

Cameron has written many books including the series of Julian Stories, Gloria Stories, and Huey Stories.

Possible Texts for Text Comparisons

There are four more books in the Julian series including *More Stories Julian Tells*; *Julian's Glorious Summer*; *Julian, Secret Agent*; and *Julian, Dream Doctor*. In addition, Cameron shares the stories of Julian's little brother Huey and his best friend Gloria in books like *The Stories Huey Tells* and *Gloria's Way*.

Cross-Curricular Connection

This book can be used in a social studies unit on trustworthiness and responsibility.

Book Summary of *The Stories Julian Tells*

Childhood is filled with both imagination and many opportunities to take on more responsibility. Cameron shares with us how Julian learns what responsibility means. Each chapter tells a different story that shines light onto the challenges of growing up, taking on more responsibility, making mistakes, and learning lessons.

- In "The Pudding Like a Night on the Sea," Julian and Huey's father makes a very special pudding for their mother. He places the responsibility of guarding the pudding with the brothers. When they eat the special pudding they were supposed to be protecting, they get a lesson in hard work and trustworthiness.

- "Catalog Cats" are special cats that come from a catalog. They will help in your garden; at least that is what Julian tells his little brother Huey. Huey can't wait for the cats to arrive in the mail. We see where Julian gets his storytelling ability as Julian's father explains catalog cats to Huey.

- In "Our Garden," Julian and Huey learn more about responsibility as their father makes them responsible for the corn and beans in the garden. From planting, to weeding, to eating, the boys learn about the rewards of responsibility and hard work.

- In "Because of Figs," Julian receives a fig tree for his birthday. He watches the tree grow and thinks that if he eats the leaves from the tree, he will grow bigger. Every time the fig tree gets new leaves, Julian eats them. He keeps getting taller but his fig tree isn't growing.

- Julian's new tooth is pushing its way in before the old tooth has fallen out. After many suggestions about how to pull out the loose tooth, Julian decides to make some money by showing "My Very Strange Teeth" to his classmates.

- Julian shares the story of meeting "Gloria Who Might Be My Best Friend." He admits to feeling a little unsure about having a girl as a best friend.

Possible Texts for Text Sets

- Cocca-Leffler, Maryann. *Princess K.I.M. and the Lie That Grew*. Albert Whitman and Co., 2009.

- Levins, Sandra. *Eli's Lie-O-Meter: A Story about Telling the Truth*. Magination Press, 2010.

- Loewen, Nancy. *We Live Here Too!: Kids Talk about Good Citizenship*. Picture Window Books, 2002.

- Stover, Jo Ann. *If Everybody Did*. JourneyForth, 1989.

- Thomson, Melissa. *Keena Ford and the Second-Grade Mix-Up*. Puffin, 2009.

Name _____ Date _____

Pre-Reading Theme Thoughts

Directions: Draw a picture of a happy face or a sad face. Your face should show how you feel about each statement. Then, use words to say what you think about each statement.

Statement	How Do You Feel? 🙂 ☹️	What Do You Think?
You always have to be responsible.		
There is a difference between lying and telling a story.		
Grownups always give kids the best advice.		
You should not make decisions about people before you get to know them.		

"The Pudding Like a Night on the Sea"

Vocabulary Overview

Key words and phrases from this section are provided below with definitions and sentences about how the words are used in the story. Introduce and discuss these important vocabulary words with the students. If you think these words or other words in the story warrant more time devoted to them, there are suggestions in the introduction for other vocabulary activities (page 5).

Word	Definition	Sentence about Text
pudding (pg. 2)	a thick, creamy dessert	Julian's father says he is going to make a special **pudding**.
windowpanes (pg. 2)	sections of glass in a window	Julian's father's laughter is like sunshine through the **windowpane**.
shiver (pg. 2)	to shake, as from cold or fear	Julian and Henry **shiver** when their father gets angry.
raft (pg. 2)	a flat structure used for transportation on the water	The pudding will taste like a **raft** of lemons floating on the ocean.
beat (pg. 3)	to stir vigorously	Julian's father has to **beat** the egg yolks.
whip (pg. 5)	to stir quickly so that air gets into the food	Julian's father has to **whip** the egg whites.
crater (pg. 8)	a round, bowl-shaped depression	If you stick your finger in the pudding, you will leave a **crater** behind.
beat (pg. 12)	to hit repeatedly	His father says it is time for Huey's **beating**.
whip (pg. 12)	to hit with an object	His father asks Julian if he is ready for his **whipping**.

Name _____ Date _____

Vocabulary Activity

Directions: Choose at least two words from the story. Draw a picture that shows what these words mean. Label your picture.

<table>
<tr><td colspan="4">Words from the Story</td></tr>
<tr><td>pudding</td><td>shiver</td><td>beat</td><td>whip</td></tr>
<tr><td>crater</td><td>windowpanes</td><td>raft</td><td></td></tr>
</table>

Directions: Answer this question.

1. Who makes a **crater** in the pudding?

_____

"The Pudding Like a Night on the Sea"

Analyzing the Literature

Provided below are discussion questions you can use in small groups, with the whole class, or for written assignments. Each question is written at two levels so that you can choose the right question for each group of students. For each question, a few key points are provided for your reference as you discuss the book with the students.

Story Element	Level 1	Level 2	Key Discussion Points
Character	How does Julian's father feel when the pudding is gone?	In the story, what emotions does Julian's father feel?	Julian's father asks the boys not to touch the pudding, and he is angry when the pudding is gone. He is also disappointed in his sons.
Character	What do Julian and Huey think about their father?	What is the relationship between Julian and Huey and their father?	Julian describes his father with love, but he also says he shivers when his father is angry.
Plot	What happens to the pudding?	Why do you think Julian's father has the boys make a new pudding?	Julian's father tells the boys not to touch the pudding, but they eat it all. Their father has them make a new pudding so they can understand and appreciate all the hard work that goes into making pudding. He is also showing them that mistakes can be fixed.
Setting	What is the setting of this story?	Describe the setting of the story.	Most of the story takes place in the kitchen. Later, their father goes to the living room, and the boys go to their bedroom.

Name _____ Date _____

Reader Response

Think

Think about a time you got into trouble. How did you change your behavior afterwards?

Narrative Writing Prompt

Write about a time when you did something you shouldn't have done. What happened and what were your consequences?

_____

_____

_____

_____

_____

_____

_____

_____

Name _____ Date _____

Guided Close Reading

Closely reread the part about Huey and Julian making the new pudding (pages 13–16).

Directions: Think about these questions. In the chart, write ideas or draw pictures as you think. Be ready to share your answers.

1. What text helps you to understand the two meanings of the words *beat* and *whip*?
2. Use the text to describe how the author uses exclamatory sentences in this section.
3. How do you feel about Julian and Huey not eating the pudding they made? Find evidence to support your thoughts.

#40103—Instructional Guide: The Stories Julian Tells   © Shell Education

Name _____ Date _____

Making Connections-Emotions

Directions: A character's feelings can change during a story. Draw three pictures that show how Julian's father felt at three different parts of the story. Next to each picture, write what he was feeling.

Name _____ Date _____

Language Learning–Figurative Language

Authors use figurative language to create more interesting ways to describe things in their stories. Here is a simile from the story: "It will taste like a whole raft of lemons."

Directions: Choose two examples of figurative language from the story. Write the examples on the lines. In each box, draw a picture that shows what the words actually say. On the lines under each box, tell what the words really mean.

_____   _____

_____   _____

_____   _____

```
┌──────────────────────┐   ┌──────────────────────┐
│                      │   │                      │
│                      │   │                      │
│                      │   │                      │
│                      │   │                      │
│                      │   │                      │
│                      │   │                      │
│                      │   │                      │
│                      │   │                      │
│                      │   │                      │
└──────────────────────┘   └──────────────────────┘
```

_____   _____

_____   _____

_____   _____

Name _____ Date _____

Story Elements-Setting

Directions: Draw a map of the kitchen. Include all the things the characters need to make the pudding. Be sure to include a key with symbols.

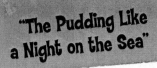

Name _____ Date _____

Story Elements-Plot

Directions: Write a recipe for fixing a mistake. You need to include the ingredients and the directions.

Ingredients

- _____
- _____
- _____
- _____
- _____

- _____
- _____
- _____
- _____
- _____

Directions

_____

_____

_____

_____

_____

_____

_____

#40103—Instructional Guide: The Stories Julian Tells

"Catalog Cats"

Vocabulary Overview

Key words and phrases from this section are provided below with definitions and sentences about how the words are used in the story. Introduce and discuss these important vocabulary words with the students. If you think these words or other words in the story warrant more time devoted to them, there are suggestions in the introduction for other vocabulary activities (page 5).

Word	Definition	Sentence about Text
catalog (pg. 17)	a book containing different items to buy	Julian's father orders a gardening **catalog**.
settled (pg. 18)	decided	When the boys say they would like to plant a garden, it is **settled**; Julian's father orders a catalog.
ordinary (pg. 19)	not exceptional in any way	Catalog cats do not act like **ordinary** cats.
invisible (pg. 26)	impossible to see	Julian's father says that catalog cats are **invisible**.
ignorant (pg. 27)	lacking in knowledge	Julian is **ignorant** for not knowing that catalog cats are invisible.
handkerchief (pg. 27)	a square piece of cloth used to wipe the eyes or nose	Huey blows his nose on his father's **handkerchief**.
backbone (pg. 28)	a series of bones down the middle of the back	If catalog cats are watching you, you can feel it in your **backbone**.
quiver (pg. 28)	to move back and forth rapidly	Being afraid can make the hair on the back of your neck **quiver**.
request (pg. 30)	to ask for	Huey **requests** a dozen catalog cats.

Name _____ Date _____

Vocabulary Activity

Directions: Draw lines to match the sentences.

Beginnings of the Sentences	Ends of the Sentences
Julian **settled** on	or they might be **invisible**.
Julian's father **orders**	and look at pictures of vegetables and flowers.
Catalog cats might be really fast	getting a huge corn plant.
They turn the pages of the **catalog**	you can **request** them.
You cannot order catalog cats but	a catalog of plants and seeds.

Directions: Answer this question.

1. Why does Huey's father hand him his **handkerchief**?

_____

_____

"Catalog Cats"

Analyzing the Literature

Provided below are discussion questions you can use in small groups, with the whole class, or for written assignments. Each question is written at two levels so you can choose the right question for each group of students. For each question, a few key points are provided for your reference as you discuss the book with the students.

Story Element	Level 1	Level 2	Key Discussion Points
Character	What does Julian's father do when Huey tells him about the catalog cats?	Why does Julian's father go along with the story of the catalog cats?	Julian's father joins in the story, furthering the tale of the catalog cats, because he wants his children to have rich imaginations and dream wonderful dreams.
Character	How does Julian stop Huey from asking their dad about the catalog cats?	Why would Huey want to learn something on his own for a change?	As the little brother, Huey is always repeating Julian. He is proud that he can learn something about catalog cats on his own.
Setting	What is the most interesting part of the setting of the story?	Describe the setting of the story.	The setting blends imagination with reality as the author and the illustrator fill the setting with catalog cats.
Plot	Why does Huey request a dozen catalog cats?	Describe what would happen if a dozen catalog cats arrive.	Huey wants to see all the catalog cats that he has been dreaming about come to life, even if they are invisible.

Name _____ Date _____

Reader Response

Think

Think about any catalogs that you have seen at your house or in a store. What is the most important part of a catalog?

Opinion Writing Prompt

Respond to this statement: *The pictures are the most important part of a catalog.*

_____

_____

_____

_____

_____

_____

_____

_____

_____

Name _____ **Date** _____

Guided Close Reading

Closely reread when Huey cries about the catalog cats
(pages 26–27).

Directions: Think about these questions. In the chart, write ideas or
draw pictures as you think. Be ready to share your answers.

1. What does it mean when the author writes, "When my father's voice gets loud, mine gets so small I can only whisper"?
2. Based on the events in the story, how much trouble is Julian in for telling Huey about the catalog cats?
3. What do you learn about Julian's father when he says, "Julian, didn't you tell Huey that catalog cats are invisible?"

Name _____ Date _____

Making Connections–Catchy Catalog . . . of Cats!

Directions: Catalogs are made to look very fancy so people will want to buy the items in them. Design a cover for a catalog of Catalog Cats. Illustrate and label the various types of catalog cats. Closely reread pages 18–19 to find out which cats are responsible for which jobs. Show different cats doing different jobs in the garden.

Name _____ Date _____

Language Learning–Writing a Friendly Letter

Directions: Write a letter to Julian, telling him how you feel about the story he told to Huey about "Catalog Cats." Do you have some advice for Julian?

Language Hints!
- Use a comma after your greeting.
- Use a comma after your closing.

_____

_____

_____

_____

_____

_____

_____

_____

_____

_____

Name _____ Date _____

Story Elements-Character

Directions: Create informative "baseball cards" for each type of catalog cat. List important information about each cat, including the job it does in the garden. Keep in mind that they are really fast.

White Cats	**Black Cats**
Yellow Cats	**Brown Cats**

#40103—Instructional Guide: The Stories Julian Tells

Name _____ Date _____

Story Elements-Plot

Directions: At the end of the story, Huey requests a dozen catalog cats. Write a story about what happens when the catalog cats arrive.

_____

_____

_____

_____

_____

_____

_____

_____

_____

_____

_____

_____

_____

_____

_____

"Our Garden" and "Because of Figs"

Vocabulary Overview

Key words and phrases from this section are provided below with definitions and sentences about how the words are used in the story. Introduce and discuss these important vocabulary words with the students. If you think these words or other words in the story warrant more time devoted to them, there are suggestions in the introduction for other vocabulary activities (page 5).

Word	Definition	Sentence About Text
genuine (pg. 32)	not fake	Julian wants to order genuine corn from the Ancients.
harvest (pg. 32)	to gather a ripened crop	Julian will need a ladder to harvest giant corn.
scarlet (pg. 32)	red	The house of flowers will be covered with scarlet blossoms.
blossom (pg. 32)	a flower on a plant	When the blossoms fall, beans begin to grow.
weed (pg. 34)	to pull out unwanted plants	Julian and Huey will weed and water their garden.
fig (pg. 37)	a tree grown for its edible fruit	Julian gets a fig tree for his birthday.
measure (pg. 39)	to determine the height of something	Julian measures himself against the mark on the wall.
spinach (pg. 40)	a plant grown for edible dark green leaves	The leaves from the fig tree taste like spinach.
fertilizer (pg. 41)	any substance used to make soil more fertile	Julian's father puts fertilizer on the fig tree to help it grow.
relax (pg. 43)	to make less taut	Julian's father relaxes his hand and lets go of the fig tree.

Name _____ Date _____

Vocabulary Activity

Directions: Each of these sentences contains a word from the stories. Cut apart these sentence strips. Put the sentences in order based on the events in the stories.

"Our Garden"

Huey plays in a house of scarlet **blossoms**.

Julian and Huey water and **weed** the garden.

Julian orders **genuine** corn of the Ancients.

"Because of Figs"

Julian begins to eat the fig tree's leaves, which taste like **spinach**.

Julian receives a **fig** tree for his birthday.

Julian's father **fertilizes** the tree.

"Our Garden" and "Because of Figs"

Analyzing the Literature

Provided below are discussion questions you can use in small groups, with the whole class, or for written assignments. Each question is written at two levels so you can choose the right question for each group of students. For each question, a few key points are provided for your reference as you discuss the book with the students.

Story Element	Level 1	Level 2	Key Discussion Points
Character	Who wants the giant corn and house of flowers?	If Julian's father didn't want the giant corn and house of flowers, why did he order them?	Julian's father wants the boys to learn to be responsible for the plants they ask for.
Plot	Why does Julian talk to the seeds?	What does Julian hope will happen when he talks to the seeds?	Julian goes outside after his bedtime because he wants to visit the new seeds. He talks to them hoping that his voice will encourage them to grow.
Character	Why does Julian want to stay taller than Huey?	What are the reasons that Julian wants to be taller?	Huey is the little brother and Julian wants to make sure he stays the big brother, older and taller.
Plot	What does Julian ask the fig tree?	The fig tree never says a word, but how does it answer Julian?	The fig tree stops growing because Julian is taking the leaves that the tree needs to create food for itself.
Plot and Science	Why isn't the fig tree growing?	Why are the new leaves important to the tree?	The tree needs leaves to complete the process of photosynthesis, turning the sun's energy into food for it to grow.

Name _____ Date _____

Reader Response

Think

Seeds need sun, water, and soil to grow. Think about what you know about planting seeds.

Informative/Explanatory Writing Prompt

Give the steps for how to plant a seed and help it grow. Draw a picture to go along with your description.

_____

_____

_____

_____

Name _____ Date _____

Guided Close Reading

Closely reread when Julian first eats the leaves (pages 40–41).

Directions: Think about these questions. In the chart, write ideas or draw pictures as you think. Be ready to share your answers.

1. Use the text to tell what two things Julian does to make sure he will grow.
2. Use this section to tell why Julian's fig tree does not grow.
3. What words in the story support the fact that Julian cares about his fig tree?

Making Connections–The Life Cycle of a Plant

Directions: A bean plant, like the one that becomes Huey's house of flowers, goes through changes in its life. It goes from bean to sprout to plant to blossom and finally to bean again. In the boxes below draw and label each stage in the life cycle of a bean plant. Cut out your drawings and give them to a friend. Have your friend place the stages in the correct order. (Number your cards lightly on the backs so that your friend can check his or her answer.)

Name _____ Date _____

Language Learning–Adjectives

Directions: The gardening catalog Julian's father requested is full of exciting descriptions and adjectives. Closely reread the page where the author describes the "corn of the Ancients" and the "house of flowers." Write and illustrate a new entry for the gardening catalog. Make up your own special plant.

Language Hints!
- Adjectives describe nouns.
- Common types of adjectives include: colors, numbers, sounds, and shapes.

_____

_____

_____

_____

_____

Name _____ Date _____

Story Elements–Characters

Directions: Julian and Huey have to work together to water and weed the garden. Write a skit including what they might say to each other while they are working.

Julian _____

_____

Huey _____

_____

Julian _____

_____

Huey _____

_____

Julian _____

_____

Huey _____

_____

Julian _____

_____

Huey _____

_____

Name _____ Date _____

Story Elements–Plot

Directions: Julian asks the fig tree if it minds that he eats its new leaves. The fig tree never answers. Draw a picture of Julian and his fig tree with a speech bubble. In the speech bubble, write what you imagine the fig tree might say to Julian.

"My Very Strange Teeth"

Vocabulary Overview

Key words and phrases from this section are provided below with definitions and sentences about how the words are used in the story. Introduce and discuss these important vocabulary words with the students. If you think these words or other words in the story warrant more time devoted to them, there are suggestions in the introduction for other vocabulary activities (page 5).

Word	Definition	Sentence about Text
wiggly (pg. 47)	moving in a twisting fashion	Julian has a **wiggly** tooth.
pliers (pg. 47)	a gripping hand tool with two hinged arms	Julian's father offers to pull out the wiggly tooth with **pliers**.
spool (pg.48)	a winder around which thread can be wrapped	Julian's father ties string from a **spool** around Julian's tooth.
thread (pg. 49)	a fine cord of twisted fibers	Julian asks his father to take the **thread** off his tooth.
method (pg. 49)	a way of doing something	Julian does not like any of his father's **methods** for pulling teeth.
prehistoric caveman (pg. 53)	a man who lived before written history	Julian's mother tells him that a **prehistoric caveman** would be happy to have teeth like his.
raw (pg. 54)	not cooked	Prehistoric cavemen ate **raw** meat.
grunt (pg. 55)	a short, deep sound	Julian **grunts** when his classmates ask about his cave-boy teeth.
mastodon (pg. 57)	an extinct elephant-like mammal	Julian's **mastodon**-eating tooth comes out when he eats an apple.

Name _____ Date _____

Vocabulary Activity

Directions: Complete each sentence below with one of the vocabulary words listed here.

Words from the Story			
grunts	wiggly	raw	method
pliers	spool	thread	prehistoric caveman

1. Julian's father ties a _____ around his tooth.

2. Julian does not want his father to use _____ to pull out his tooth.

3. When the children ask about Julian's tooth, he _____ so they cannot see in his mouth.

4. Julian's _____ tooth comes out when he bites into an apple.

Directions: Answer this question.

5. Why does Julian ask his father if he knows another **method** for removing teeth?

_____

_____

"My Very Strange Teeth"

Analyzing the Literature

Provided below are discussion questions you can use in small groups, with the whole class, or for written assignments. Each question is written at two levels so you can choose the right question for each group of students. For each question, a few key points are provided for your reference as you discuss the book with the students.

Story Element	Level 1	Level 2	Key Discussion Points
Character	Why does Julian's father offer to pull out his wiggly tooth?	Why does Julian's father continue to offer different methods of dealing with a loose tooth?	Julian's father wants to help Julian, but his father also wants Julian to have some say in what happens to his tooth.
Character	What does Julian's mother say about his tooth?	Why does Julian's mother say that prehistoric cavemen would be happy to have his teeth?	Julian's mother does not want him to feel bad about his two teeth or to get his feelings hurt if he gets teased.
Setting	Describe the two settings in this story.	How is the setting from this story different from the other stories in the book?	This is the only story with a setting outside Julian's house or neighborhood.
Plot	How much money does Julian make from showing his cave-boy teeth?	How does Julian's plan to make money fall apart?	After only one showing, Julian's tooth comes out on its own when he bites into an apple. He only makes one cent.

Name _____ Date _____

Reader Response

Think

Think about your teeth. Do you remember when you lost your first tooth?

Narrative Writing Prompt

Write a story about your teeth. You can write about having loose teeth or about losing teeth.

_____

_____

_____

_____

_____

_____

_____

_____

_____

_____

_____

Name _____ Date _____

Guided Close Reading

Closely reread the part where Julian's dad offers to help
Julian pull out his loose tooth (pages 47–51).

Directions: Think about these questions. In the chart, write ideas or
draw pictures as you think. Be ready to share your answers.

1. How does the author describe Julian's very strange teeth?
2. Use the text to describe the methods Julian's father wants to use to remove Julian's loose tooth.
3. According to the story, what is Julian's concern with each of his father's methods?

Name _____ Date _____

Making Connections-Take Care of Your Teeth!

Directions: Having a healthy smile means you take good care of your teeth. Use the toothbrush below to show what you know about taking care of your teeth. On the handle write, "Have a Healthy Smile." On each bristle write a way to care for your teeth. For example, you could write "flossing" on one bristle.

Language Learning—Parts of Speech

Directions: Invent a machine to pull out loose teeth. Draw and label your machine. Below your picture, summarize how the machine works. In your labels and descriptions, use at least 5 nouns and 5 verbs.

> **Language Hints!**
> - Nouns name people, places, things, or ideas.
> - Verbs are action words.

_____

_____

_____

_____

_____

Name _____ Date _____

Story Elements–Characters

Directions: Make a poster advertising Julian's exhibit of his very strange teeth. Be sure to include Julian in the poster.

Name _____ **Date** _____

"My Very Strange Teeth"

Story Elements–Plot

Directions: Create a cartoon strip showing the different ways that Julian's father tries to pull out Julian's loose tooth.

"Gloria Who Might Be My Best Friend"

Vocabulary Overview

Key words and phrases from this section are provided below with definitions and sentences about how the words are used in the story. Introduce and discuss these important vocabulary words with the students. If you think these words or other words in the story warrant more time devoted to them, there are suggestions in the introduction for other vocabulary activities (page 5).

word	Definition	Sentence about Text
braided (pg. 60)	a hairdo formed by twisting the hair	Gloria's hair is **braided.**
pigtails (pg. 60)	hair collected on both sides of the head	Gloria has **pigtails** tied with red ribbons.
cartwheel (pg. 60)	a sideways handspring with arms and legs extended	Julian tries to do a **cartwheel** like Gloria, but he falls.
branch (pg. 62)	a division of the main stem of the plant	Gloria climbs on a **branch** to look in the nest.
squawked (pg. 62)	a harsh, abrupt scream	The robin **squawks** at them when they are near the nest.
mustache (pg. 63)	a stain on the upper lip	The strawberry drink leaves a red **mustache** on his lips.
fasten (pg. 67)	to attach to	They **fasten** their wishes to the tail of the kite.
beyond (pg. 69)	on the far side of	They fly their kites in the field **beyond** Julian's house.

Name _____ Date _____

Vocabulary Activity

Directions: Practice your vocabulary and writing skills. Write at least four sentences using words from the story. Make sure your sentences show what the words mean.

Words from the Story			
braided	pigtails	cartwheel	branch
squawked	mustache	fasten	beyond

_____

_____

_____

_____

_____

_____

_____

Directions: Answer this question.

1. Why does the mother robin **squawk** at Gloria?

_____

_____

"Gloria Who Might Be My Best Friend"

Analyzing the Literature

Provided below are discussion questions you can use in small groups, with the whole class, or for written assignments. Each question is written at two levels so you can choose the right question for each group of students. For each question, a few key points are provided for your reference as you discuss the book with the students.

Story Element	Level 1	Level 2	Key Discussion Points
Character	Why doesn't Julian want a girl for a friend?	Describe what Gloria does to make Julian want to be friends.	When Gloria does not make fun of him, he decides that she will be his friend.
Character	What does Gloria do when Julian tries to do a cartwheel?	Why doesn't Gloria laugh when Julian tries a cartwheel?	Gloria understands that to be good at something it takes practice and encouragement.
Setting	Where do they go to fly their kite?	Why do they go beyond the house to fly the kite?	Julian's yard has trees, a house of flowers, and a garage. There isn't room to fly a kite in his yard.
Plot	What does Julian wish for?	What do you think Gloria wishes for?	Julian makes five wishes, and we know what they are (page 66). Gloria keeps her two wishes a secret.

Name _____ Date _____

Reader Response

Think

Think about your friends. What characteristics do your best friends have?

Opinion Writing Prompt

Who would you rather spend time with, Julian or Gloria? Write about what you might do together.

_____

_____

_____

_____

_____

_____

_____

_____

_____

Name _____ Date _____

Guided Close Reading

Closely reread when Julian meets Gloria (pages 60–62).

Directions: Think about these questions. In the chart, write ideas or draw pictures as you think. Be ready to share your answers.

1. What words in the text describe Julian's cartwheel? Retell what happened in your own words.
2. According to the story, when did Julian decide he could be friends with Gloria?
3. What in the text tells you what kind of friend Gloria will be?

Name _____ Date _____

Making Connections—Like a Diamond in the Sky

Directions: A diamante poem is a poem made of seven lines. When it is written, it looks like a diamond. A diamond is similar to the shape of a kite. Use the guidelines below to write a diamante poem about Julian and Gloria.

Julian

_____
Write 2 adjectives that describe Julian.

_____
Write 3 verbs that Julian does.

_____
Write 4 nouns that both Julian and Gloria have.

_____
Write 3 verbs that Gloria does.

_____
Write 2 adjectives that describe Gloria.

Gloria

Name _____ Date _____

Language Learning–Spelling

Directions: The words on this page are all found in this section of *The Stories Julian Tells*. Some of the words are spelled wrong below. Check the spelling of each word. Write the correct spelling next to any misspelled words. Then, rewrite the words in alphabetical order.

Language Hints!
- Start alphabetizing with the first letter of each word.
- Compare words from left to right as you alphabetize.

Words from the Section	Alphabetize
braided	_____
pigtales	_____
cartwheel	_____
branch	_____
sqwawked	_____
mustach	_____
beyond	_____
fasteen	_____

Name _____ Date _____

Story Elements-Setting

Directions: Draw an image that shows Julian and Gloria flying their kite. Draw the picture from the kite's point of view above them.

Name _____ Date _____

Story Elements-Plot

Directions: Design your own wish kite. In the sky around the kite, draw symbols and images that represent you. On the tail write three wishes that you have.

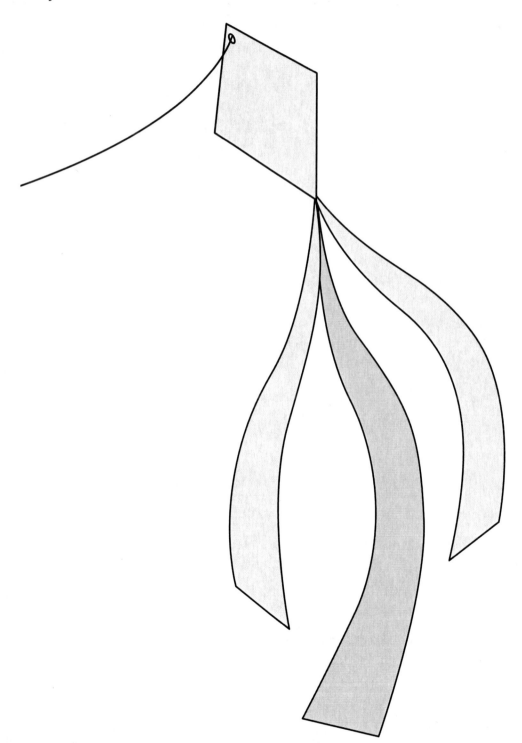

Name _____ Date _____

Post-Reading Theme Thoughts

Directions: Choose a main character from *The Stories Julian Tells*. Pretend you are that character. Draw a picture of a happy face or a sad face to show how the character would feel about each statement. Then explain why.

Character I Chose: _____

Statement	How does the character feel? ☺ ☹	Why does the character feel this way?
You always have to be responsible.		
There is a difference between lying and telling a story.		
Grownups always give kids the best advice.		
You should not make decisions about people before you get to know them.		

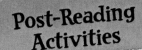
Name _____ Date _____

Culminating Activity: Reader's Theater

Directions: Turn your classroom into Julian's garden! Look at the beautiful illustrations in the book. How can you create the setting of the garden in your class? Don't forget to include the scarlet blossoms of the house of flowers and at least one catalog cat! When you have a wonderful setting created, act out this reader's theater with two friends. You can even write a script of your own describing another adventure for Julian and Huey.

The Wish Kite
Characters: Julian, Huey, Narrator

Narrator: Julian and Huey finish weeding and watering the garden. They are sitting in the house of flowers drinking lemonade.

Julian: I wish something exciting would happen.

Huey: I wish for ice cream.

Julian: I wish for lemon pudding, like a whole raft of lemons.

Huey: Just wishing won't make it happen.

Julian: Oh, yeah? I know how we can make our wishes come true. Come on!

Narrator: The boys head to the garage.

Huey: What are you doing? Where are you going?

Julian: Just wait. Let me get everything.

Huey: Are you looking for a catalog cat? Do they make wishes come true?

Julian: Of course not, silly, they are too busy in the garden to bother with wishes.

Huey: Then how can our wishes come true?

Culminating Activity: Reader's Theater (cont.)

Julian: A wishing kite!

Huey: A wishing kite? You're making that up!

Julian: Nope. They're real. I'll show you how to make one.

Narrator: Julian shows Huey how to build a kite out of sticks and newspaper.

Julian: Now it's time to write down our wishes. Don't tell me what your wishes are, or they might not come true.

Huey: I'm not very good at spelling.

Julian: I don't think spelling counts when you're wishing.

Narrator: Julian shows Huey how to fasten the wishes to the tail of the kite, and the boys head beyond the house to fly their wish kite.

Julian: Wow, Huey! Our wishes are really flying! I bet you wished to see catalog cats.

Huey: I'm not telling!

Julian: Let's pull the kite back in.

Huey: Why? This is fun!

Julian: We have to check the tail. If all the wishes are gone, they will come true.

Narrator: The boys pulled the kite back in. Sure enough, all the wishes were gone.

Huey: That was fun! How did you learn to make wish kites?

Julian: My best friend taught me.

Culminating Activity: Reader's Theater (cont.)

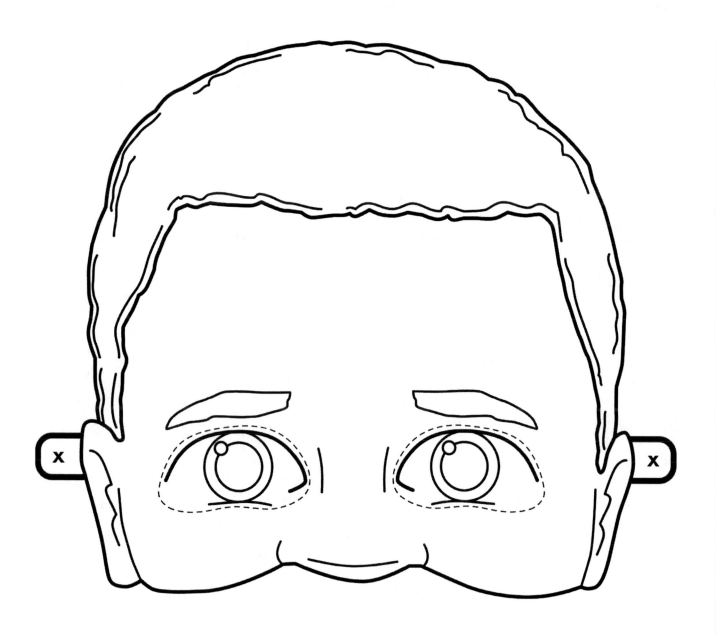

Julian

Culminating Activity: Reader's Theater (cont.)

Huey

Name _____ Date _____

Comprehension Assessment

Directions: Fill in the bubble for the best response to each question.

"The Pudding Like a Night on the Sea"

1. What was the purpose of Julian's father having the boys make a new pudding?

    (A) He is too tired from making the first one.

    (B) Mom is hungry and has nothing to eat.

    (C) He wants to teach them that a mistake can be fixed.

    (D) He thinks making pudding is fun.

"Catalog Cats"

2. What does it show about Huey's father when he does not say that there are no such things as catalog cats?

    (E) He knows Huey will cry harder if he finds out about catalog cats.

    (F) He wants Huey to believe in magical, wonderful things.

    (G) He wants Huey to respect his big brother.

    (H) The catalog cats would be angry.

"Our Garden" and "Because of Figs"

3. What does Julian hope to gain from eating the new leaves off the fig tree?

    (A) He can't wait for the figs.

    (B) He hopes they will make him grow like they make the fig tree grow.

    (C) He thinks they taste great.

    (D) He hopes he will be able to see the catalog cats if he eats the leaves.

Comprehension Assessment (cont.)

"My Very Strange Teeth"

4. Describe the ways that Julian's father and mother each try to make him feel better.

_____

_____

_____

_____

_____

_____

_____

"Gloria Who Might Be My Best Friend"

5. What event in the story makes Julian change his mind about not wanting a girl for a best friend?

(E) Gloria only wants to do girl stuff.

(F) Gloria gives him her bike.

(G) Rather than laugh, Gloria encourages him when he falls doing a cartwheel.

(H) Gloria laughs at him when he falls over trying to do a cartwheel.

Name _____ Date _____

Response to Literature: Learning Valuable Lessons

Directions: Childhood is filled with both imagination and many opportunities to take on more responsibility. Each section of this book tells a different story that shines light on the challenges of growing up, taking on more responsibility, making mistakes, and learning lessons. Choose one story and compare and contrast the lesson Julian learns with what you've learned in your life. Complete the Venn diagram below. Then, answer the questions on the next page.

Story Title: _____

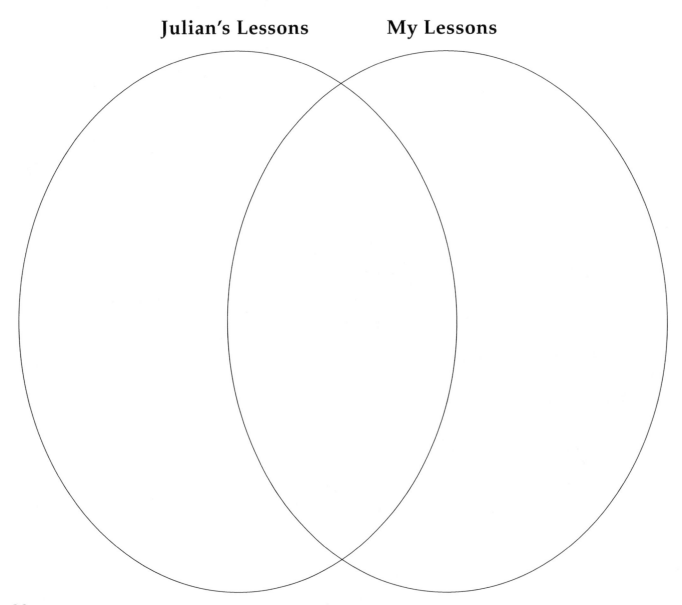

Julian's Lessons   My Lessons

Name _____ Date _____

Response to Literature: Learning Valuable Lessons (cont.)

1. How will Julian's lesson help him to be more responsible in the future?

_____

_____

_____

_____

2. How has your lesson helped to make you more responsible?

_____

_____

_____

_____

3. What does your lesson and Julian's have in common?

_____

_____

_____

_____

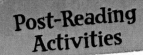

Name _____ Date _____

Response to Literature Rubric

Directions: Use this rubric to evaluate student responses.

Great Job	Good Work	Keep Trying
☐ You answered all three questions completely. You included many details.	☐ You answered all three questions.	☐ You did not answer all three questions.
☐ Your handwriting is very neat. There are no spelling errors.	☐ Your handwriting can be neater. There are some spelling errors.	☐ Your handwriting is not very neat. There are many spelling errors.
☐ Your picture is neat and fully colored.	☐ Your picture is neat and some of it is colored.	☐ Your picture is not very neat and/or fully colored.
☐ Creativity is clear in both the picture and the writing.	☐ Creativity is clear in either the picture or the writing.	☐ There is not much creativity in either the picture or the writing.

Teacher Comments: _____

_____

_____

 #40103—Instructional Guide: The Stories Julian Tells

The responses provided here are just examples of what students may answer. Many accurate responses are possible for the questions throughout this unit.

Vocabulary Activity—Section 1:
"A Pudding Like a Night on the Sea" (page 15)

1. Huey makes the **crater** in the pudding.

Analyzing the Literature—Section 1:
"A Pudding Like a Night on the Sea" (page 18)

1. "Now it's your time for beating!" makes us think the father will hit Huey. Then he hands him the egg beater. "I hope you're ready for some whipping!" makes us think the father is going to hit Julian. Then, he hands him the egg whites and tell him to start whipping . . . the egg whites.

2. Almost every sentence Julian's father utters is an exclamatory sentence. This tells us a lot about this exuberant, larger-than-life character.

3. Huey says it is hard work beating the eggs. Julian says his arm hurts from whipping. After all their hard work, they are too tired to enjoy the pudding.

Language Learning—Section 1:
"A Pudding Like a Night on the Sea" (page 20)

- "When he laughs, the sun laughs in the windowpanes." His laughter brings joy to others.
- "It will taste like a whole raft of lemons." The pudding will taste like lemons.
- "It will taste like a night on the sea." The pudding will be smooth.
- "It looked like craters on the moon." The pudding had holes in the surface.

Vocabulary Activity—Section 2:
"Catalog Cats" (page 24)

- Julian's father **orders** a catalog of plants and seeds.
- Catalog cats might be really fast or they might be **invisible**.
- They turn the pages of the **catalog** and look at pictures of vegetables and flowers.
- You cannot order catalog cats but you can **request** them.

1. Huey's father hands him a **handkerchief** so Huey can blow his nose.

Guided Close Reading—Section 2: "Catalog Cats" (page 27)

1. When Julian's father gets angry, it makes Julian feel very small and weak.

2. Julian's father plays along with the story, even adding some more details of his own. Julian will not get in trouble for this imaginative tale.

3. In this one statement, he makes Huey feel better and lets him know that, while Julian is the big brother, he doesn't know everything.

Vocabulary Activity—Section 3:
"Our Garden" and "Because of Figs" (page 33)

- **"Our Garden"**—Julian orders **genuine** corn of the Ancients. Julian and Huey water and **weed** the garden. Huey plays in a house of scarlet **blossoms.**
- **"Because of Figs"**—Julian receives a **fig** tree for his birthday. Julian begins to eat the fig tree's leaves, which taste like **spinach**. Julian's father **fertilizes** the tree.

Guided Close Reading: Section 3:
"Our Garden" and "Because of Figs" (page 36)

1. Julian eats the new leaves off the fig tree and does a little dance.

2. The tree did not grow because Julian eats all of the new leaves off the tree. It can't perform photosynthesis.

3. Julian asks the fig tree if it minds if he eats its leaves.

Vocabulary Activity—Section 4:
"My Very Strange Teeth" (page 42)

1. Julian's father ties a **thread** around his tooth.

2. Julian does not want his father to use **pliers** to pull out his tooth.

3. When the children ask about Julian's tooth, he **grunts** so they cannot see in his mouth.

4. Julian's **wiggly** tooth comes out when he bites into an apple.

5. Julian does not like any of the **methods** his father suggests. He thinks they will hurt.

Guided Close Reading—Section 4:
"My Very Strange Teeth" (page 45)

1. Julian has two right bottom teeth, one wiggly old one and one new one.

2. He will pull it out with a pair of pliers. He will tie a string to the tooth and the other end to a door, which he will slam hard. He also suggests Julian just keep pushing it around with his finger until it comes out.

3. Julian worries about how much it will hurt.

Vocabulary Activity—Section 5:
"Gloria Who Might Be My Best Friend" (page 51)

1. The mother robin **squawks** to warn them to stay away from her nest.

Guided Close Reading—Section 5:
"Gloria Who Might Be My Best Friend" (page 54)

1. Julian's hands go down and his feet go up, and then he falls over.

2. Julian decides that he can be friends with Gloria when she does not laugh at him for his attempt at a cartwheel.

3. Gloria will be a supportive friend because she says encouraging things like, "It takes practice."

Making Connections—Section 5:
"Gloria Who Might Be My Best Friend" (page 55)

This diamante can be used as an example if your students have trouble writing their own.

Julian
Curious   Funny
Wishing   Writing   Drinking
Kite   Mustaches   Wishes   Friend
Cartwheeling   Giggling
Friendly   Thoughtful
Gloria

Language Learning—Section 5:
"Gloria Who Might Be My Best Friend" (page 56)

beyond, braided, branch, cartwheel, fasten, mustache, pigtails, squawked

Comprehension Assessment
(pages 64–65)

1. C. He wants to teach them that a mistake can be fixed.

2. F. He wants Huey to believe in magical, wonderful things.

3. B. He hopes they will make him grow like they made the fig tree grow.

4. Julian's father wants to help Julian feel better by getting the wiggly tooth out. Julian's mother wants to help Julian feel better by telling him that his teeth are special, and they would be would be the envy of cavemen.

5. G. Rather than laugh, Gloria encourages him when he falls doing a cartwheel.